Be Still
in the Presence
of the LORD
and wait patiently
for him to act.

— PSALM 37:7 —

This Journal Belongs To

_____

Verse:_____   Date: ___/___/___

Devotion Time

_____
_____
_____
_____
_____
_____
_____
_____
_____
_____
_____
_____
_____
_____
_____
_____
_____

Reflections

I am Grateful for:
_____
_____
_____
_____
_____

I know God is in my life because:
_____
_____
_____
_____

Memory Verse:
_____
_____
_____
_____

My Prayer List:
_____
_____
_____
_____
_____

Verse:_____   Date: ___/___/___

Devotion Time

_____
_____
_____
_____
_____
_____
_____
_____
_____
_____
_____
_____
_____
_____
_____
_____
_____
_____
_____
_____

Reflections

I am Grateful for:
_____
_____
_____
_____
_____
_____

I know God is in my life because:
_____
_____
_____
_____
_____
_____
_____

Memory Verse:
_____
_____
_____
_____
_____

My Prayer List:
_____
_____
_____
_____

Verse:_____ Date: ___/___/___

Devotion Time

_____
_____
_____
_____
_____
_____
_____
_____
_____
_____
_____
_____
_____
_____
_____
_____
_____
_____
_____
_____
_____

Reflections

I am Grateful for:
_____
_____
_____
_____
_____

I know God is in my life because:
_____
_____
_____
_____
_____

Memory Verse:
_____
_____
_____
_____

My Prayer List:
_____
_____
_____
_____
_____

Verse:_____ Date: ___/___/___

Devotion Time

_____
_____
_____
_____
_____
_____
_____
_____
_____
_____
_____
_____
_____
_____
_____
_____
_____

Reflections

I am Grateful for:
_____
_____
_____
_____
_____
_____

I know God is in my life because:
_____
_____
_____
_____
_____

Memory Verse:
_____
_____
_____
_____
_____

My Prayer List:
_____
_____
_____
_____
_____

Verse:_____ Date: ___/___/___

Devotion Time

_____
_____
_____
_____
_____
_____
_____
_____
_____
_____
_____
_____
_____
_____
_____
_____
_____
_____

I am Grateful for:
_____
_____
_____
_____

I know God is in my life because:
_____
_____
_____
_____

Memory Verse:
_____
_____
_____
_____

Reflections

My Prayer List:
_____
_____
_____
_____
_____

Verse:_____   Date: ___/___/___

Devotion Time

_____
_____
_____
_____
_____
_____
_____
_____
_____
_____
_____
_____
_____
_____
_____
_____
_____
_____
_____

Reflections

I am Grateful for:
_____
_____
_____
_____
_____
_____

I know God is in my life because:
_____
_____
_____
_____
_____

Memory Verse:
_____
_____
_____
_____

My Prayer List:
_____
_____
_____
_____
_____

Verse:_____   Date: __/__/__

Devotion Time

_____
_____
_____
_____
_____
_____
_____
_____
_____
_____
_____
_____
_____
_____
_____
_____
_____
_____
_____

I am Grateful for:
_____
_____
_____
_____
_____
_____

I know God is in my life because:
_____
_____
_____
_____
_____

Memory Verse:
_____
_____
_____
_____
_____

Reflections

My Prayer List:
_____
_____
_____
_____
_____
_____

Verse:_____   Date: ___/___/___

Devotion Time

_____
_____
_____
_____
_____
_____
_____
_____
_____
_____
_____
_____
_____
_____
_____
_____
_____
_____
_____
_____

Reflections

I am Grateful for:
_____
_____
_____
_____
_____

I know God is in my life because:
_____
_____
_____
_____

Memory Verse:
_____
_____
_____
_____

My Prayer List:
_____
_____
_____
_____

Verse:_____   Date: __/__/__

Devotion Time

_____
_____
_____
_____
_____
_____
_____
_____
_____
_____
_____
_____
_____
_____
_____
_____
_____
_____

Reflections

I am Grateful for:_____
_____
_____
_____
_____
_____

I know God is in my life because:___
_____
_____
_____
_____
_____

Memory Verse:_____
_____
_____
_____
_____

My Prayer List:_____
_____
_____
_____
_____
_____
_____

Verse:_____   Date: ___/___/___

Devotion Time

_____
_____
_____
_____
_____
_____
_____
_____
_____
_____
_____
_____
_____
_____
_____
_____
_____
_____
_____

Reflections

I am Grateful for:
_____
_____
_____
_____
_____
_____

I know God is in my life because:
_____
_____
_____
_____
_____

Memory Verse:
_____
_____
_____
_____
_____
_____

My Prayer List:
_____
_____
_____
_____
_____

Verse:_____   Date: ___/___/___

Devotion Time

_____
_____
_____
_____
_____
_____
_____
_____
_____
_____
_____
_____
_____
_____
_____
_____
_____
_____
_____

Reflections

I am Grateful for:
_____
_____
_____
_____
_____

I know God is in my life because:
_____
_____
_____
_____

Memory Verse:
_____
_____
_____
_____
_____

My Prayer List:
_____
_____
_____
_____
_____

Verse:_____   Date: ___/___/___

Devotion Time

_____
_____
_____
_____
_____
_____
_____
_____
_____
_____
_____
_____
_____
_____
_____
_____
_____
_____

Reflections

I am Grateful for:
_____
_____
_____
_____
_____
_____
_____
_____

I know God is in my life because:
_____
_____
_____
_____
_____

Memory Verse:
_____
_____
_____
_____
_____

My Prayer List:
_____
_____
_____
_____
_____

Verse:_____   Date: __/__/__

Devotion Time

_____
_____
_____
_____
_____
_____
_____
_____
_____
_____
_____
_____
_____
_____
_____
_____
_____
_____

Reflections

I am Grateful for:
_____
_____
_____
_____
_____

I know God is in my life because:
_____
_____
_____
_____

Memory Verse:
_____
_____
_____
_____

My Prayer List:
_____
_____
_____
_____
_____

Verse:_____   Date: ___/___/___

Devotion Time

_____
_____
_____
_____
_____
_____
_____
_____
_____
_____
_____
_____
_____
_____
_____
_____
_____
_____
_____

Reflections

I am Grateful for:
_____
_____
_____
_____
_____

I know God is in my life because:
_____
_____
_____
_____

Memory Verse:
_____
_____
_____
_____

My Prayer List:
_____
_____
_____
_____
_____

Verse:_____   Date: ___/___/___

Devotion Time

_____
_____
_____
_____
_____
_____
_____
_____
_____
_____
_____
_____
_____
_____
_____
_____
_____
_____
_____
_____

Reflections

I am Grateful for:
_____
_____
_____
_____
_____
_____

I know God is in my life because:
_____
_____
_____
_____
_____
_____

Memory Verse:
_____
_____
_____
_____

My Prayer List:
_____
_____
_____
_____
_____

Verse:_____   Date: ___/___/___

Devotion Time

_____
_____
_____
_____
_____
_____
_____
_____
_____
_____
_____
_____
_____
_____
_____
_____
_____
_____

Reflections

I am Grateful for:
_____
_____
_____
_____
_____
_____

I know God is in my life because:
_____
_____
_____
_____
_____

Memory Verse:
_____
_____
_____
_____
_____

My Prayer List:
_____
_____
_____
_____
_____
_____

Verse:_____   Date: ___/___/___

Devotion Time

_____
_____
_____
_____
_____
_____
_____
_____
_____
_____
_____
_____
_____
_____
_____
_____
_____
_____
_____

I am Grateful for:
_____
_____
_____
_____
_____
_____

I know God is in my life because:
_____
_____
_____
_____
_____
_____

Memory Verse:
_____
_____
_____
_____
_____

My Prayer List:
_____
_____
_____
_____
_____
_____

Reflections

Verse:_____ Date: ___/___/___

Devotion Time

_____
_____
_____
_____
_____
_____
_____
_____
_____
_____
_____
_____
_____
_____
_____
_____
_____
_____
_____

Reflections

I am Grateful for:
_____
_____
_____
_____
_____
_____

I know God is in my life because:
_____
_____
_____
_____
_____
_____

Memory Verse:
_____
_____
_____
_____

My Prayer List:
_____
_____
_____
_____
_____

Verse:_____ Date: __/__/__

Devotion Time

_____
_____
_____
_____
_____
_____
_____
_____
_____
_____
_____
_____
_____
_____
_____
_____
_____
_____

Reflections

I am Grateful for:
_____
_____
_____
_____
_____
_____

I know God is in my life because:
_____
_____
_____
_____
_____

Memory Verse:
_____
_____
_____
_____
_____

My Prayer List:
_____
_____
_____
_____
_____

Verse:_____ Date: __/__/__

Devotion Time

_____
_____
_____
_____
_____
_____
_____
_____
_____
_____
_____
_____
_____
_____
_____
_____
_____
_____
_____
_____
_____

Reflections

I am Grateful for:
_____
_____
_____
_____
_____

I know God is in my life because:
_____
_____
_____
_____
_____

Memory Verse:
_____
_____
_____
_____
_____

My Prayer List:
_____
_____
_____
_____
_____

Verse:_____ Date: ___/___/___

Devotion Time

_____

_____

_____

_____

_____

_____

_____

_____

_____

_____

_____

_____

_____

_____

_____

_____

I am Grateful for:
_____

_____

_____

_____

_____

I know God is in my life because:
_____

_____

_____

_____

Memory Verse:
_____

_____

_____

_____

My Prayer List:
_____

_____

_____

_____

_____

Reflections

Verse:_____   Date: ___/___/___

Devotion Time

_____
_____
_____
_____
_____
_____
_____
_____
_____
_____
_____
_____
_____
_____
_____
_____
_____
_____
_____

Reflections

I am Grateful for:
_____
_____
_____
_____
_____
_____

I know God is in my life because:
_____
_____
_____
_____
_____

Memory Verse:
_____
_____
_____
_____
_____

My Prayer List:
_____
_____
_____
_____
_____
_____

Verse:_____   Date: ___/___/___

Devotion Time

_____

_____

_____

_____

_____

_____

_____

_____

_____

_____

_____

_____

_____

_____

_____

_____

_____

_____

I am Grateful for:
_____

_____

_____

_____

_____

_____

I know God is in my life because:
_____

_____

_____

_____

_____

Memory Verse:
_____

_____

_____

_____

_____

Reflections

My Prayer List:
_____

_____

_____

_____

_____

Verse:_____   Date: ___/___/___

Devotion Time

_____
_____
_____
_____
_____
_____
_____
_____
_____
_____
_____
_____
_____
_____
_____
_____
_____
_____
_____
_____
_____
_____

Reflections

I am Grateful for:
_____
_____
_____
_____
_____

I know God is in my life because:
_____
_____
_____
_____
_____

Memory Verse:
_____
_____
_____
_____

My Prayer List:
_____
_____
_____
_____
_____

Verse:_____   Date: ___/___/___

Devotion Time

_____
_____
_____
_____
_____
_____
_____
_____
_____
_____
_____
_____
_____
_____
_____
_____
_____
_____
_____

Reflections

I am Grateful for:
_____
_____
_____
_____
_____
_____

I know God is in my life because:
_____
_____
_____
_____
_____
_____

Memory Verse:
_____
_____
_____
_____
_____

My Prayer List:
_____
_____
_____
_____
_____

Verse:_____   Date: ___/___/___

Devotion Time

_____
_____
_____
_____
_____
_____
_____
_____
_____
_____
_____
_____
_____
_____
_____
_____
_____
_____
_____

Reflections

I am Grateful for:
_____
_____
_____
_____
_____

I know God is in my life because:
_____
_____
_____
_____
_____

Memory Verse:
_____
_____
_____
_____

My Prayer List:
_____
_____
_____
_____
_____

Verse:_____   Date: ___/___/___

Devotion Time

_____
_____
_____
_____
_____
_____
_____
_____
_____
_____
_____
_____
_____
_____
_____
_____
_____
_____
_____

Reflections

I am Grateful for:
_____
_____
_____
_____
_____
_____

I know God is in my life because:
_____
_____
_____
_____
_____

Memory Verse:
_____
_____
_____
_____

My Prayer List:
_____
_____
_____
_____
_____
_____

Verse:_____   Date: ___/___/___

Devotion Time

_____
_____
_____
_____
_____
_____
_____
_____
_____
_____
_____
_____
_____
_____
_____
_____
_____
_____
_____
_____

Reflections

I am Grateful for:
_____
_____
_____
_____
_____
_____

I know God is in my life because:
_____
_____
_____
_____
_____

Memory Verse:
_____
_____
_____
_____

My Prayer List:
_____
_____
_____
_____
_____

Verse:_____   Date: ___/___/___

Devotion Time

_____
_____
_____
_____
_____
_____
_____
_____
_____
_____
_____
_____
_____
_____
_____
_____
_____
_____
_____
_____
_____

Reflections

I am Grateful for:
_____
_____
_____
_____
_____
_____

I know God is in my life because:
_____
_____
_____
_____
_____
_____

Memory Verse:
_____
_____
_____
_____
_____

My Prayer List:
_____
_____
_____
_____
_____

Verse:_____   Date: ___/___/___

Devotion Time

_____
_____
_____
_____
_____
_____
_____
_____
_____
_____
_____
_____
_____
_____
_____
_____
_____
_____
_____

Reflections

I am Grateful for:
_____
_____
_____
_____
_____
_____

I know God is in my life because:
_____
_____
_____
_____
_____
_____

Memory Verse:
_____
_____
_____
_____
_____

My Prayer List:
_____
_____
_____
_____
_____

Verse:_____   Date: __/__/__

Devotion Time

_____
_____
_____
_____
_____
_____
_____
_____
_____
_____
_____
_____
_____
_____
_____
_____
_____
_____
_____

Reflections

I am Grateful for:
_____
_____
_____
_____
_____
_____

I know God is in my life because:
_____
_____
_____
_____
_____
_____

Memory Verse:
_____
_____
_____
_____

My Prayer List:
_____
_____
_____
_____
_____
_____

Verse:_____   Date: ___/___/___

Devotion Time

_____
_____
_____
_____
_____
_____
_____
_____
_____
_____
_____
_____
_____
_____
_____
_____
_____
_____
_____

Reflections

I am Grateful for:
_____
_____
_____
_____
_____

I know God is in my life because:
_____
_____
_____
_____
_____

Memory Verse:
_____
_____
_____
_____

My Prayer List:
_____
_____
_____
_____

Verse:_____   Date: __/__/__

Devotion Time

_____

_____

_____

_____

_____

_____

_____

_____

_____

_____

_____

_____

_____

_____

_____

_____

_____

_____

Reflections

I am Grateful for:

_____

_____

_____

_____

_____

I know God is in my life because:

_____

_____

_____

_____

Memory Verse:

_____

_____

_____

_____

My Prayer List:

_____

_____

_____

_____

_____

Verse:_____ Date: ___/___/___

Devotion Time

_____
_____
_____
_____
_____
_____
_____
_____
_____
_____
_____
_____
_____
_____
_____
_____
_____
_____
_____
_____
_____

Reflections

I am Grateful for:
_____
_____
_____
_____
_____
_____
_____

I know God is in my life because:
_____
_____
_____
_____
_____

Memory Verse:
_____
_____
_____
_____
_____

My Prayer List:
_____
_____
_____
_____
_____

Verse:_____ Date: ___/___/___

Devotion Time

_____
_____
_____
_____
_____
_____
_____
_____
_____
_____
_____
_____
_____
_____
_____
_____
_____
_____
_____
_____

Reflections

I am Grateful for:
_____
_____
_____
_____
_____

I know God is in my life because:
_____
_____
_____
_____
_____

Memory Verse:
_____
_____
_____

My Prayer List:
_____
_____
_____
_____
_____

Verse: _____   Date: ___/___/___

Devotion Time

_____
_____
_____
_____
_____
_____
_____
_____
_____
_____
_____
_____
_____
_____
_____
_____
_____
_____
_____
_____

Reflections

I am Grateful for:
_____
_____
_____
_____
_____
_____

I know God is in my life because:
_____
_____
_____
_____
_____
_____

Memory Verse:
_____
_____
_____
_____
_____

My Prayer List:
_____
_____
_____
_____
_____

Verse:_____   Date: __/__/__

Devotion Time

_____
_____
_____
_____
_____
_____
_____
_____
_____
_____
_____
_____
_____
_____
_____
_____
_____
_____
_____

Reflections

I am Grateful for:
_____
_____
_____
_____
_____
_____

I know God is in my life because:
_____
_____
_____
_____
_____

Memory Verse:
_____
_____
_____
_____

My Prayer List:
_____
_____
_____
_____
_____

Verse:_____   Date: ___/___/___

Devotion Time

_____

_____

_____

_____

_____

_____

_____

_____

_____

_____

_____

_____

_____

_____

_____

_____

_____

_____

I am Grateful for:

_____

_____

_____

_____

_____

_____

I know God is in my life because:

_____

_____

_____

_____

_____

Memory Verse:

_____

_____

_____

_____

_____

My Prayer List:

_____

_____

_____

_____

_____

Reflections

Verse:_____   Date: ___/___/___

Devotion Time

_____
_____
_____
_____
_____
_____
_____
_____
_____
_____
_____
_____
_____
_____
_____
_____
_____
_____
_____

Reflections

I am Grateful for:
_____
_____
_____
_____
_____

I know God is in my life because:
_____
_____
_____
_____
_____

Memory Verse:
_____
_____
_____
_____

My Prayer List:
_____
_____
_____
_____
_____

Verse:_____   Date: ___/___/___

Devotion Time

_____
_____
_____
_____
_____
_____
_____
_____
_____
_____
_____
_____
_____
_____
_____
_____
_____
_____
_____

Reflections

I am Grateful for:
_____
_____
_____
_____
_____
_____

I know God is in my life because:
_____
_____
_____
_____
_____
_____

Memory Verse:
_____
_____
_____
_____
_____

My Prayer List:
_____
_____
_____
_____
_____
_____

Verse:_____   Date: __/__/__

Devotion Time

_____
_____
_____
_____
_____
_____
_____
_____
_____
_____
_____
_____
_____
_____
_____
_____
_____
_____
_____
_____

I am Grateful for:
_____
_____
_____
_____
_____
_____

I know God is in my life because:
_____
_____
_____
_____
_____

Memory Verse:
_____
_____
_____
_____
_____

Reflections

My Prayer List:
_____
_____
_____
_____
_____
_____

Verse:_____ Date: ___/___/___

Devotion Time

_____
_____
_____
_____
_____
_____
_____
_____
_____
_____
_____
_____
_____
_____
_____
_____
_____
_____

I am Grateful for:
_____
_____
_____
_____
_____

I know God is in my life because:
_____
_____
_____
_____
_____

Memory Verse:
_____
_____
_____
_____

My Prayer List:
_____
_____
_____
_____
_____

Reflections

Verse:_____   Date: __/__/__

Devotion Time

_____
_____
_____
_____
_____
_____
_____
_____
_____
_____
_____
_____
_____
_____
_____
_____
_____
_____

Reflections

I am Grateful for:
_____
_____
_____
_____
_____
_____

I know God is in my life because:
_____
_____
_____
_____
_____

Memory Verse:
_____
_____
_____
_____
_____

My Prayer List:
_____
_____
_____
_____
_____

Verse:_____ Date: ___/___/___

Devotion Time

_____
_____
_____
_____
_____
_____
_____
_____
_____
_____
_____
_____
_____
_____
_____
_____
_____
_____
_____
_____

Reflections

I am Grateful for:
_____
_____
_____
_____
_____

I know God is in my life because:
_____
_____
_____
_____
_____

Memory Verse:
_____
_____
_____
_____

My Prayer List:
_____
_____
_____
_____
_____

Verse:_____ Date: __/__/__

Devotion Time

_____
_____
_____
_____
_____
_____
_____
_____
_____
_____
_____
_____
_____
_____
_____
_____
_____
_____
_____

Reflections

I am Grateful for:
_____
_____
_____
_____
_____

I know God is in my life because:
_____
_____
_____
_____

Memory Verse:
_____
_____
_____
_____

My Prayer List:
_____
_____
_____
_____
_____

Verse:_____   Date: ___/___/___

Devotion Time

_____
_____
_____
_____
_____
_____
_____
_____
_____
_____
_____
_____
_____
_____
_____
_____
_____
_____

Reflections

I am Grateful for:
_____
_____
_____
_____
_____

I know God is in my life because:
_____
_____
_____
_____

Memory Verse:
_____
_____
_____
_____

My Prayer List:
_____
_____
_____
_____

Verse:_____   Date: ___/___/___

Devotion Time

_____
_____
_____
_____
_____
_____
_____
_____
_____
_____
_____
_____
_____
_____
_____
_____
_____
_____
_____

Reflections

I am Grateful for: _____
_____
_____
_____
_____
_____
_____

I know God is in my life because:
_____
_____
_____
_____
_____

Memory Verse: _____
_____
_____
_____
_____

My Prayer List: _____
_____
_____
_____
_____
_____

Verse:_____   Date: ___/___/___

Devotion Time

_____
_____
_____
_____
_____
_____
_____
_____
_____
_____
_____
_____
_____
_____
_____
_____
_____
_____
_____

Reflections

I am Grateful for:
_____
_____
_____
_____
_____
_____

I know God is in my life because:
_____
_____
_____
_____
_____

Memory Verse:
_____
_____
_____
_____
_____

My Prayer List:
_____
_____
_____
_____
_____

Verse:_____   Date: __/__/__

Devotion Time

_____
_____
_____
_____
_____
_____
_____
_____
_____
_____
_____
_____
_____
_____
_____
_____
_____
_____
_____

Reflections

I am Grateful for:
_____
_____
_____
_____
_____
_____

I know God is in my life because:
_____
_____
_____
_____
_____

Memory Verse:
_____
_____
_____
_____
_____

My Prayer List:
_____
_____
_____
_____
_____

Verse:_____   Date: ___/___/___

Devotion Time

_____
_____
_____
_____
_____
_____
_____
_____
_____
_____
_____
_____
_____
_____
_____
_____
_____
_____
_____

Reflections

I am Grateful for:
_____
_____
_____
_____
_____
_____

I know God is in my life because:
_____
_____
_____
_____
_____
_____

Memory Verse:
_____
_____
_____
_____
_____

My Prayer List:
_____
_____
_____
_____
_____

Verse:_____   Date: ___/___/___

Devotion Time

_____
_____
_____
_____
_____
_____
_____
_____
_____
_____
_____
_____
_____
_____
_____
_____
_____
_____
_____
_____

Reflections

I am Grateful for:
_____
_____
_____
_____
_____

I know God is in my life because:
_____
_____
_____
_____

Memory Verse:
_____
_____
_____
_____

My Prayer List:
_____
_____
_____
_____
_____

Verse:_____   Date: __/__/__

Devotion Time

_____
_____
_____
_____
_____
_____
_____
_____
_____
_____
_____
_____
_____
_____
_____
_____
_____

I am Grateful for:
_____
_____
_____
_____
_____

I know God is in my life because:
_____
_____
_____
_____
_____

Memory Verse:
_____
_____
_____
_____

Reflections

My Prayer List:
_____
_____
_____
_____
_____

Verse:_____   Date: ___/___/___

Devotion Time

_____
_____
_____
_____
_____
_____
_____
_____
_____
_____
_____
_____
_____
_____
_____
_____
_____
_____
_____

Reflections

I am Grateful for:
_____
_____
_____
_____
_____
_____

I know God is in my life because:
_____
_____
_____
_____
_____

Memory Verse:
_____
_____
_____
_____

My Prayer List:
_____
_____
_____
_____
_____

Verse:_____   Date: ___/___/___

Devotion Time

_____
_____
_____
_____
_____
_____
_____
_____
_____
_____
_____
_____
_____
_____
_____
_____
_____
_____

I am Grateful for:
_____
_____
_____
_____
_____

I know God is in my life because:
_____
_____
_____
_____
_____

Memory Verse:
_____
_____
_____
_____

Reflections

My Prayer List:
_____
_____
_____
_____

Verse:_____   Date: __/__/__

Devotion Time

_____
_____
_____
_____
_____
_____
_____
_____
_____
_____
_____
_____
_____
_____
_____
_____
_____
_____

I am Grateful for:
_____
_____
_____
_____
_____
_____

I know God is in my life because:
_____
_____
_____
_____
_____

Memory Verse:
_____
_____
_____
_____

Reflections

My Prayer List:
_____
_____
_____
_____
_____
_____

Verse:_____   Date: ___/___/___

Devotion Time

_____
_____
_____
_____
_____
_____
_____
_____
_____
_____
_____
_____
_____
_____
_____
_____
_____
_____

Reflections

I am Grateful for:
_____
_____
_____
_____
_____

I know God is in my life because:
_____
_____
_____
_____
_____
_____

Memory Verse:
_____
_____
_____
_____

My Prayer List:
_____
_____
_____
_____
_____

Verse:_____   Date: ___/___/___

Devotion Time

_____
_____
_____
_____
_____
_____
_____
_____
_____
_____
_____
_____
_____
_____
_____
_____
_____
_____
_____
_____

Reflections

I am Grateful for:
_____
_____
_____
_____
_____

I know God is in my life because:
_____
_____
_____
_____

Memory Verse:
_____
_____
_____
_____

My Prayer List:
_____
_____
_____
_____
_____

Verse:_____   Date: ___/___/___

Devotion Time

_____
_____
_____
_____
_____
_____
_____
_____
_____
_____
_____
_____
_____
_____
_____
_____
_____
_____
_____
_____

Reflections

I am Grateful for:
_____
_____
_____
_____
_____
_____

I know God is in my life because:
_____
_____
_____
_____
_____
_____

Memory Verse:
_____
_____
_____
_____
_____

My Prayer List:
_____
_____
_____
_____
_____
_____

Verse:_____   Date: __/__/__

Devotion Time

_____
_____
_____
_____
_____
_____
_____
_____
_____
_____
_____
_____
_____
_____
_____
_____
_____
_____
_____

Reflections

I am Grateful for:
_____
_____
_____
_____
_____

I know God is in my life because:
_____
_____
_____
_____
_____

Memory Verse:
_____
_____
_____
_____

My Prayer List:
_____
_____
_____
_____
_____

Verse:_____   Date: __/__/__

Devotion Time

_____
_____
_____
_____
_____
_____
_____
_____
_____
_____
_____
_____
_____
_____
_____
_____
_____
_____
_____
_____

Reflections

I am Grateful for:
_____
_____
_____
_____
_____

I know God is in my life because:
_____
_____
_____
_____
_____

Memory Verse:
_____
_____
_____
_____

My Prayer List:
_____
_____
_____
_____
_____

Verse:_____ Date: ___/___/___

Devotion Time

_____
_____
_____
_____
_____
_____
_____
_____
_____
_____
_____
_____
_____
_____
_____
_____
_____
_____
_____

Reflections

I am Grateful for:
_____
_____
_____
_____
_____
_____

I know God is in my life because:
_____
_____
_____
_____
_____

Memory Verse:
_____
_____
_____
_____
_____

My Prayer List:
_____
_____
_____
_____
_____

Verse:_____   Date: ___/___/___

Devotion Time

_____
_____
_____
_____
_____
_____
_____
_____
_____
_____
_____
_____
_____
_____
_____
_____
_____
_____
_____
_____

Reflections

I am Grateful for:
_____
_____
_____
_____
_____
_____

I know God is in my life because:
_____
_____
_____
_____
_____

Memory Verse:
_____
_____
_____
_____

My Prayer List:
_____
_____
_____
_____
_____

Verse:_____   Date: __/__/__

Devotion Time

_____
_____
_____
_____
_____
_____
_____
_____
_____
_____
_____
_____
_____
_____
_____
_____
_____
_____
_____
_____

Reflections

I am Grateful for:
_____
_____
_____
_____
_____
_____

I know God is in my life because:
_____
_____
_____
_____
_____
_____

Memory Verse:
_____
_____
_____
_____
_____

My Prayer List:
_____
_____
_____
_____
_____

Verse:_____   Date: ___/___/___

Devotion Time

_____
_____
_____
_____
_____
_____
_____
_____
_____
_____
_____
_____
_____
_____
_____
_____
_____
_____

Reflections

I am Grateful for:
_____
_____
_____
_____
_____
_____

I know God is in my life because:
_____
_____
_____
_____
_____

Memory Verse:
_____
_____
_____
_____

My Prayer List:
_____
_____
_____
_____

Verse:_____ Date: __/__/__

Devotion Time

_____
_____
_____
_____
_____
_____
_____
_____
_____
_____
_____
_____
_____
_____
_____
_____
_____
_____
_____

I am Grateful for:
_____
_____
_____
_____
_____

I know God is in my life because:
_____
_____
_____
_____
_____

Memory Verse:
_____
_____
_____
_____

My Prayer List:
_____
_____
_____
_____
_____

Reflections

Verse:_____   Date: ___/___/___

Devotion Time

_____
_____
_____
_____
_____
_____
_____
_____
_____
_____
_____
_____
_____
_____
_____
_____
_____
_____
_____

Reflections

I am Grateful for:
_____
_____
_____
_____
_____

I know God is in my life because:
_____
_____
_____
_____

Memory Verse:
_____
_____
_____
_____

My Prayer List:
_____
_____
_____
_____
_____
_____

Verse:_____   Date: ___/___/___

Devotion Time

_____
_____
_____
_____
_____
_____
_____
_____
_____
_____
_____
_____
_____
_____
_____
_____
_____

Reflections

I am Grateful for:
_____
_____
_____
_____
_____
_____

I know God is in my life because:
_____
_____
_____
_____
_____

Memory Verse:
_____
_____
_____
_____

My Prayer List:
_____
_____
_____
_____
_____

Verse:_____   Date: ___/___/___

Devotion Time

_____
_____
_____
_____
_____
_____
_____
_____
_____
_____
_____
_____
_____
_____
_____
_____
_____

Reflections

I am Grateful for:
_____
_____
_____
_____
_____
_____

I know God is in my life because:
_____
_____
_____
_____
_____

Memory Verse:
_____
_____
_____
_____
_____

My Prayer List:
_____
_____
_____
_____
_____

Verse:_____   Date: ___/___/___

Devotion Time

_____
_____
_____
_____
_____
_____
_____
_____
_____
_____
_____
_____
_____
_____
_____
_____
_____
_____

I am Grateful for:
_____
_____
_____
_____
_____

I know God is in my life because:
_____
_____
_____
_____

Memory Verse:
_____
_____
_____
_____

Reflections

My Prayer List:
_____
_____
_____
_____
_____

Verse:_____   Date: ___/___/___

Devotion Time

_____
_____
_____
_____
_____
_____
_____
_____
_____
_____
_____
_____
_____
_____
_____
_____
_____
_____

Reflections

I am Grateful for:
_____
_____
_____
_____
_____
_____

I know God is in my life because:
_____
_____
_____
_____
_____
_____

Memory Verse:
_____
_____
_____
_____
_____

My Prayer List:
_____
_____
_____
_____
_____

Verse:_____ Date: ___/___/___

Devotion Time

_____
_____
_____
_____
_____
_____
_____
_____
_____
_____
_____
_____
_____
_____
_____
_____
_____
_____
_____
_____
_____

Reflections

I am Grateful for:
_____
_____
_____
_____
_____

I know God is in my life because:
_____
_____
_____
_____

Memory Verse:
_____
_____
_____
_____

My Prayer List:
_____
_____
_____
_____

Verse:_____   Date: __/__/__

Devotion Time

_____
_____
_____
_____
_____
_____
_____
_____
_____
_____
_____
_____
_____
_____
_____
_____
_____
_____

Reflections

I am Grateful for: _____
_____
_____
_____
_____
_____

I know God is in my life because: ___
_____
_____
_____
_____
_____

Memory Verse: _____
_____
_____
_____
_____

My Prayer List: _____
_____
_____
_____
_____
_____

Verse:_____ Date: ___/___/___

Devotion Time

_____
_____
_____
_____
_____
_____
_____
_____
_____
_____
_____
_____
_____
_____
_____
_____
_____

Reflections

I am Grateful for:
_____
_____
_____
_____
_____

I know God is in my life because:
_____
_____
_____
_____

Memory Verse:
_____
_____
_____
_____

My Prayer List:
_____
_____
_____
_____

Verse:_____   Date: ___/___/___

Devotion Time

_____
_____
_____
_____
_____
_____
_____
_____
_____
_____
_____
_____
_____
_____
_____
_____
_____
_____
_____
_____

I am Grateful for:
_____
_____
_____
_____
_____

I know God is in my life because:
_____
_____
_____
_____

Memory Verse:
_____
_____
_____
_____

My Prayer List:
_____
_____
_____
_____
_____
_____

Reflections

Verse:_____   Date: __/__/__

Devotion Time

_____

_____

_____

_____

_____

_____

_____

_____

_____

_____

_____

_____

_____

_____

_____

_____

_____

_____

_____

_____

_____

I am Grateful for:

_____

_____

_____

_____

_____

I know God is in my life because:

_____

_____

_____

_____

Memory Verse:

_____

_____

_____

_____

Reflections

My Prayer List:

_____

_____

_____

_____

_____

Verse:_____   Date: __/__/__

Devotion Time

_____
_____
_____
_____
_____
_____
_____
_____
_____
_____
_____
_____
_____
_____
_____
_____
_____
_____

Reflections

I am Grateful for:
_____
_____
_____
_____
_____

I know God is in my life because:
_____
_____
_____
_____
_____

Memory Verse:
_____
_____
_____
_____

My Prayer List:
_____
_____
_____
_____
_____

Verse:_____   Date: __/__/__

Devotion Time

_____
_____
_____
_____
_____
_____
_____
_____
_____
_____
_____
_____
_____
_____
_____
_____
_____
_____

Reflections

I am Grateful for:
_____
_____
_____
_____
_____

I know God is in my life because:
_____
_____
_____
_____

Memory Verse:
_____
_____
_____
_____

My Prayer List:
_____
_____
_____
_____
_____

Verse:_____   Date: ___/___/___

Devotion Time

_____
_____
_____
_____
_____
_____
_____
_____
_____
_____
_____
_____
_____
_____
_____
_____
_____
_____
_____

Reflections

I am Grateful for:
_____
_____
_____
_____
_____

I know God is in my life because:
_____
_____
_____
_____
_____

Memory Verse:
_____
_____
_____
_____

My Prayer List:
_____
_____
_____
_____
_____

Verse:_____   Date: ___/___/___

Devotion Time

_____
_____
_____
_____
_____
_____
_____
_____
_____
_____
_____
_____
_____
_____
_____
_____
_____
_____

Reflections

I am Grateful for:
_____
_____
_____
_____
_____
_____
_____

I know God is in my life because:
_____
_____
_____
_____
_____

Memory Verse:
_____
_____
_____
_____
_____

My Prayer List:
_____
_____
_____
_____
_____

Verse:_____ Date: __/__/__

Devotion Time

_____
_____
_____
_____
_____
_____
_____
_____
_____
_____
_____
_____
_____
_____
_____
_____
_____
_____
_____

I am Grateful for:
_____
_____
_____
_____
_____
_____

I know God is in my life because:
_____
_____
_____
_____
_____
_____

Memory Verse:
_____
_____
_____
_____

My Prayer List:
_____
_____
_____
_____
_____

Reflections

Verse:_____   Date: ___/___/___

Devotion Time

_____

_____

_____

_____

_____

_____

_____

_____

_____

_____

_____

_____

_____

_____

_____

_____

_____

I am Grateful for:

_____

_____

_____

_____

_____

I know God is in my life because:

_____

_____

_____

_____

Memory Verse:

_____

_____

_____

_____

My Prayer List:

_____

_____

_____

_____

_____

Reflections

Verse:_____ Date: ___/___/___

Devotion Time

_____
_____
_____
_____
_____
_____
_____
_____
_____
_____
_____
_____
_____
_____
_____
_____
_____

Reflections

I am Grateful for:
_____
_____
_____
_____
_____
_____

I know God is in my life because:
_____
_____
_____
_____
_____

Memory Verse:
_____
_____
_____
_____

My Prayer List:
_____
_____
_____
_____
_____

Verse:_____   Date: ___/___/___

Devotion Time

_____
_____
_____
_____
_____
_____
_____
_____
_____
_____
_____
_____
_____
_____
_____
_____
_____
_____
_____
_____

Reflections

I am Grateful for:_____
_____
_____
_____
_____

I know God is in my life because:
_____
_____
_____
_____

Memory Verse:_____
_____
_____
_____

My Prayer List:_____
_____
_____
_____
_____
_____

Verse:_____   Date: ___/___/___

Devotion Time

_____
_____
_____
_____
_____
_____
_____
_____
_____
_____
_____
_____
_____
_____
_____
_____
_____
_____

Reflections

I am Grateful for:
_____
_____
_____
_____
_____
_____

I know God is in my life because:
_____
_____
_____
_____
_____

Memory Verse:
_____
_____
_____
_____

My Prayer List:
_____
_____
_____
_____
_____

Verse:_____   Date: ___/___/___

Devotion Time

_____

_____

_____

_____

_____

_____

_____

_____

_____

_____

_____

_____

_____

_____

_____

_____

_____

Reflections

I am Grateful for:
_____

_____

_____

_____

_____

_____

I know God is in my life because:
_____

_____

_____

_____

_____

Memory Verse:
_____

_____

_____

_____

_____

My Prayer List:
_____

_____

_____

_____

_____

Verse:_____ Date: ___/___/___

Devotion Time

_____
_____
_____
_____
_____
_____
_____
_____
_____
_____
_____
_____
_____
_____
_____
_____
_____
_____
_____
_____

Reflections

I am Grateful for:
_____
_____
_____
_____
_____
_____

I know God is in my life because:
_____
_____
_____
_____

Memory Verse:
_____
_____
_____
_____
_____

My Prayer List:
_____
_____
_____
_____
_____

Verse:_____   Date: __/__/__

Devotion Time

_____

I am Grateful for:
_____
_____
_____
_____
_____
_____

_____

I know God is in my life because:
_____
_____
_____
_____
_____

Memory Verse:
_____
_____
_____

Reflections

My Prayer List:
_____
_____
_____
_____
_____

Verse:_____   Date: ___/___/___

Devotion Time

_____
_____
_____
_____
_____
_____
_____
_____
_____
_____
_____
_____
_____
_____
_____
_____
_____
_____

Reflections

I am Grateful for:
_____
_____
_____
_____
_____
_____

I know God is in my life because:
_____
_____
_____
_____
_____

Memory Verse:
_____
_____
_____
_____
_____

My Prayer List:
_____
_____
_____
_____
_____

Verse:_____   Date: __/__/__

Devotion Time

_____
_____
_____
_____
_____
_____
_____
_____
_____
_____
_____
_____
_____
_____
_____
_____
_____
_____

Reflections

I am Grateful for:
_____
_____
_____
_____
_____

I know God is in my life because:
_____
_____
_____
_____

Memory Verse:
_____
_____
_____
_____

My Prayer List:
_____
_____
_____
_____

Verse:_____   Date: __/__/__

Devotion Time

_____
_____
_____
_____
_____
_____
_____
_____
_____
_____
_____
_____
_____
_____
_____
_____
_____
_____
_____
_____

Reflections

I am Grateful for:
_____
_____
_____
_____
_____
_____

I know God is in my life because:
_____
_____
_____
_____
_____

Memory Verse:
_____
_____
_____
_____

My Prayer List:
_____
_____
_____
_____

Verse:_____   Date: __/__/__

Devotion Time

_____
_____
_____
_____
_____
_____
_____
_____
_____
_____
_____
_____
_____
_____
_____
_____

Reflections

I am Grateful for:
_____
_____
_____
_____
_____

I know God is in my life because:
_____
_____
_____
_____

Memory Verse:
_____
_____
_____
_____

My Prayer List:
_____
_____
_____
_____
_____

Verse:_____ Date: __/__/__

Devotion Time

_____
_____
_____
_____
_____
_____
_____
_____
_____
_____
_____
_____
_____
_____
_____
_____
_____
_____
_____

Reflections

I am Grateful for:
_____
_____
_____
_____
_____
_____

I know God is in my life because:
_____
_____
_____
_____
_____

Memory Verse:
_____
_____
_____
_____
_____

My Prayer List:
_____
_____
_____
_____
_____
_____

Verse:_____   Date: ___/___/___

Devotion Time

_____
_____
_____
_____
_____
_____
_____
_____
_____
_____
_____
_____
_____
_____
_____
_____
_____
_____

Reflections

I am Grateful for:
_____
_____
_____
_____
_____
_____

I know God is in my life because:
_____
_____
_____
_____
_____

Memory Verse:
_____
_____
_____
_____
_____

My Prayer List:
_____
_____
_____
_____
_____

Verse:_____   Date: ___/___/___

Devotion Time

_____
_____
_____
_____
_____
_____
_____
_____
_____
_____
_____
_____
_____
_____
_____
_____
_____
_____

Reflections

I am Grateful for:
_____
_____
_____
_____
_____
_____

I know God is in my life because:
_____
_____
_____
_____
_____

Memory Verse:
_____
_____
_____
_____
_____

My Prayer List:
_____
_____
_____
_____
_____

Verse:_____   Date: ___/___/___

Devotion Time

_____
_____
_____
_____
_____
_____
_____
_____
_____
_____
_____
_____
_____
_____
_____
_____
_____
_____
_____
_____

Reflections

I am Grateful for:
_____
_____
_____
_____
_____
_____

I know God is in my life because:
_____
_____
_____
_____
_____

Memory Verse:
_____
_____
_____
_____

My Prayer List:
_____
_____
_____
_____

Verse:_____   Date: ___/___/___

Devotion Time

_____
_____
_____
_____
_____
_____
_____
_____
_____
_____
_____
_____
_____
_____
_____
_____
_____
_____
_____
_____

Reflections

I am Grateful for:
_____
_____
_____
_____
_____

I know God is in my life because:
_____
_____
_____
_____
_____

Memory Verse:
_____
_____
_____
_____

My Prayer List:
_____
_____
_____
_____
_____

Verse:_____ Date: ___/___/___

Devotion Time

_____
_____
_____
_____
_____
_____
_____
_____
_____
_____
_____
_____
_____
_____
_____
_____
_____

Reflections

I am Grateful for:
_____
_____
_____
_____
_____
_____

I know God is in my life because:
_____
_____
_____
_____
_____

Memory Verse:
_____
_____
_____
_____
_____

My Prayer List:
_____
_____
_____
_____
_____

Verse:_____   Date: __/__/__

Devotion Time

_____
_____
_____
_____
_____
_____
_____
_____
_____
_____
_____
_____
_____
_____
_____
_____
_____
_____

Reflections

I am Grateful for:
_____
_____
_____
_____
_____
_____

I know God is in my life because:
_____
_____
_____
_____
_____

Memory Verse:
_____
_____
_____
_____
_____

My Prayer List:
_____
_____
_____
_____
_____

Verse:_____   Date: ___/___/___

Devotion Time

_____
_____
_____
_____
_____
_____
_____
_____
_____
_____
_____
_____
_____
_____
_____
_____
_____
_____

Reflections

I am Grateful for:
_____
_____
_____
_____
_____

I know God is in my life because:
_____
_____
_____
_____

Memory Verse:
_____
_____
_____
_____

My Prayer List:
_____
_____
_____
_____

Verse:_____   Date: ___/___/___

Devotion Time

_____
_____
_____
_____
_____
_____
_____
_____
_____
_____
_____
_____
_____
_____
_____
_____
_____
_____
_____
_____

Reflections

I am Grateful for:
_____
_____
_____
_____
_____
_____

I know God is in my life because:
_____
_____
_____
_____
_____

Memory Verse:
_____
_____
_____
_____

My Prayer List:
_____
_____
_____
_____
_____

Made in the USA
Las Vegas, NV
02 May 2024

89466734R00056